LACROSSE
FOR FUN!

By Sandra Will

Content Adviser: Tavius Cheatham, Associate Physical Education Director, Barnard College, New York City, New York

Reading Adviser: Frances J. Bonacci, Ed.D., Reading Specialist, Cambridge, Massachusetts

COMPASS POINT BOOKS
MINNEAPOLIS, MINNESOTA

Compass Point Books
3109 West 50th Street, #115
Minneapolis, MN 55410

Visit Compass Point Books on the Internet at www.compasspointbooks.com
or e-mail your request to custserv@compasspointbooks.com

Editors: Deb Berry and Aubrey Whitten/Bill SMITH STUDIO; and Shelly Lyons
Designer/Page Production: Geron Hoy, Kavita Ramchandran, Sinae Sohn, Marina Terletsky, and Brock Waldron/Bill SMITH STUDIO
Photo Researcher: Jacqueline Lissy Brustein, Scott Rosen, and Allison Smith/Bill SMITH STUDIO
Art Director: Jaime Martens
Creative Director: Keith Griffin
Editorial Director: Carol Jones
Managing Editor: Catherine Neitge

Library of Congress Cataloging-in-Publication Data
Will, Sandra.
  Lacrosse for fun! / by Sandra Will.
    p. cm. -- (Sports for fun!)
  Includes bibliographical references and index.
  ISBN 0-7565-1685-4 (hard cover)
  1. Lacrosse--Juvenile literature. I. Title. II. Series.
  GV989.14.W55 2006
  796.347--dc22
                          2005025222

Printed in the United States of America.

Table of Contents

● ●

Note: In this book, there are two kinds of vocabulary words. Lacrosse Words to Know are words specific to lacrosse. They are defined on page 46. Other Words to Know are helpful words that aren't related only to lacrosse. They are defined on page 47.

Over the Centuries

Did you know that lacrosse is considered to be North America's first sport? The game of lacrosse traces its roots back to many Native American tribes. The Native Americans created "the little brother of war," which is now known as lacrosse. The game was often played to resolve conflicts, heal the sick, and develop strong men. In 1636, a Frenchman first documented the game in Canada and named it lacrosse. By the 1800s, it was a popular game played among French pioneers in Canada and the United States. Over time, more and more people began to play lacrosse.

Originally, only men played lacrosse. In 1890, the first women's lacrosse game was played in Scotland. Both men's and women's lacrosse were played under the same rules until the 1930s, when the men's game began to change. Today, men's and women's lacrosse are played with different rules.

It has also become one of the fastest growing team sports in the United States.

Goal of the Game

Both men's and women's lacrosse are team sports. The object of the game is to shoot the ball into the opponent's goal and score more goals, or points, than the other team. Each team scores goals by shooting the ball into the opposing team's net. The goalkeeper, or goalie, tries to stop the ball from entering the net.

Sizing Up the Turf

Men's lacrosse is usually played outdoors on a field, which is why the sport is commonly called field lacrosse. The field is made of grass or artificial turf and looks a lot like a football or soccer field. Outdoor lacrosse fields measure 110 yards (100 meters) long and 60 yards (55 m) wide. The midline divides the field in half. The endline marks the boundary of the field on each end. Two restraining lines, which are 35 yards (32 m) from each endline, mark the offensive and defensive zones that surround each goal. Look at the diagram to learn the names and different parts of the men's outdoor lacrosse field.

Lacrosse can also be played indoors. Indoor lacrosse is known as box lacrosse. The playing field for box lacrosse is smaller than that used for field lacrosse. It is also played in an arena on a field made of artificial turf. Field and box lacrosse also have different rules. This book focuses on outdoor field lacrosse.

endlines

sidelines

restraining line

goal

crease

crease

goal

goal line

midline

goal line

restraining line

Let's Hear It for the Boys!

All men's lacrosse games are divided into quarters. The length of the game depends on the level. College games last 60 minutes and have 15-minute quarters. High school games are usually 48 minutes long, with 12-minute quarters. In youth lacrosse, the games last 32 minutes, with eight-minute quarters. All men's field lacrosse games have a two-minute break between the first and second quarters and third and fourth quarters. A 10-minute halftime divides the game.

The game begins with a face-off at midfield. The referee places the ball between the raised sticks of two players and blows the whistle to begin play. Each face-off player tries to control the ball and gain possession for their team. Referees also hold face-offs after a goal is scored and to begin each quarter.

During the game, each team is allowed to have 10 players on the field: a goalie, three defensemen, three midfielders, and three attackmen. The players use different skills and strategies to move the ball around the field, score goals, and try to win the game.

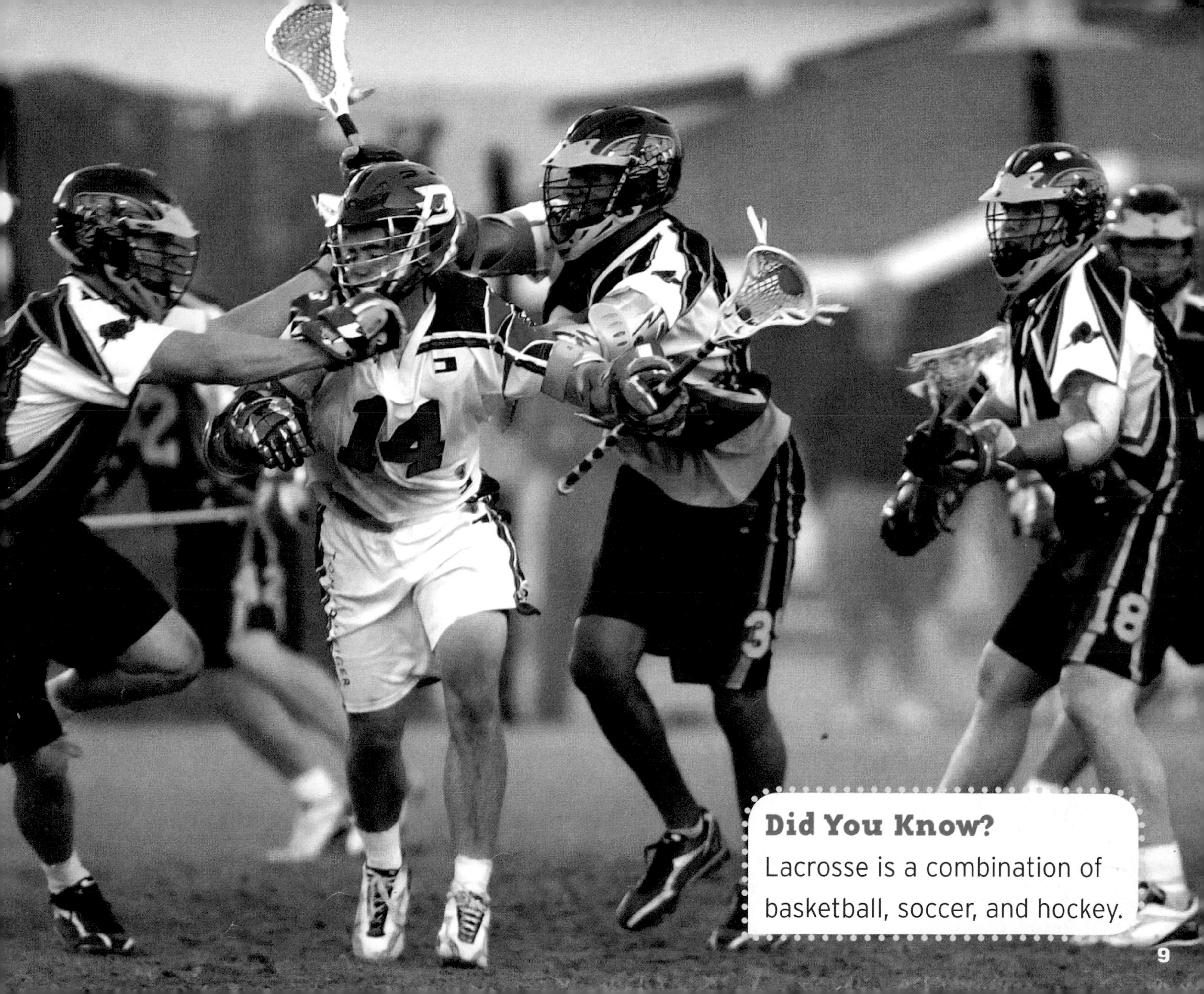

Did You Know?

Lacrosse is a combination of basketball, soccer, and hockey.

Suit Up!

Men's lacrosse is a contact sport, which means players can hit or charge into each other's bodies. This contact game requires special equipment that keeps players safe and healthy, and helps them play the game.

Shoulder pads, arm pads, and rib pads are worn by men's lacrosse players to protect them from injury.

Players wear padded gloves that protect their hands from injury.

All men's players must wear a helmet that has a face mask, chin pad, and chin strap.

Crosses, or lacrosse sticks, are made of plastic and lightweight metal. They have a shaped net pocket at the end that allows players to catch the ball.

The ball is made of solid rubber and can be white, yellow, or orange. It weighs about 5 ounces (140 grams) and is approximately 8 inches (20 centimeters) around.

Special shoes called cleats help players grip the field easily and prevent slipping and falling.

Protect Those Pearly Whites!
Mouthpieces protect a player's teeth and are mandatory. They must be a bright color so the referee can see them.

On the Attack

The offense moves the ball toward its opponent's goal and scores. Field lacrosse has two types of offensive positions:

Attack: The attackman's main responsibility is to score goals. He usually plays in the offensive end of the field. A good attackman protects the stick with his hands and has quick feet to move around the goal and score.

Midfield: A midfielder covers the entire field, playing both offense and defense. The midfielder clears the ball from the defense to the attack and moves the ball up the field. Because midfielders must run the field so much, they need to be in good shape. They should be speedy and able to change directions quickly.

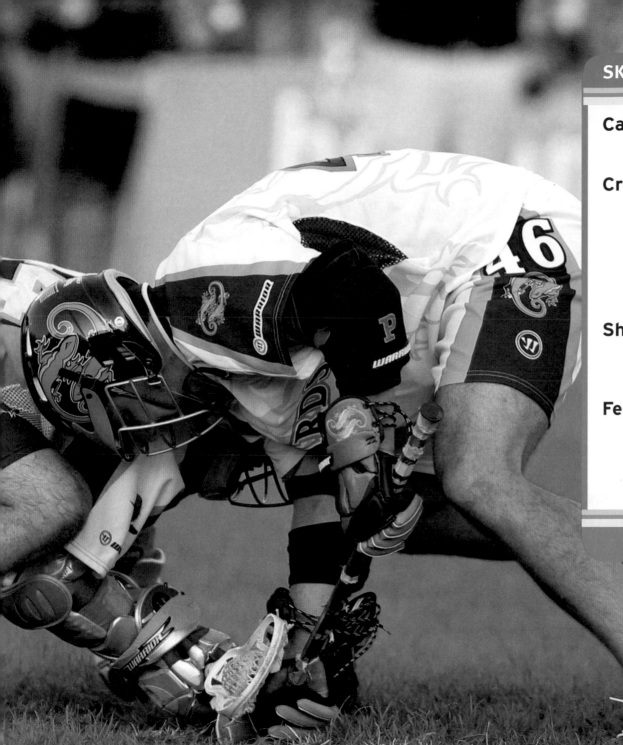

SKILL	DESCRIPTION
Catching	receiving a passed ball with the stick
Cradling	keeping the ball secure in the pocket of the crosse to be passed or shot while running
Shooting	aiming the ball at the goal and trying to score
Feeding	passing the ball to a teammate who is in position for a shot at the goal

Block That Ball!

Defense is an important part of winning lacrosse games. A strong defense prevents the opponent from scoring and gains control of the ball. Here are the two defensive positions in men's lacrosse:

Defenseman: The defenseman's responsibility is to defend the goal. He plays in the defensive half of the field. Good defensemen must be able to react quickly during the game. They must also be aggressive.

Goalkeeper: The goalkeeper, or goalie, protects the goal and stops the opposing team from scoring. The goalie also helps direct the defensemen on the field. The best goalies have good coordination and quickness, so they can block fast shots.

Do Not Enter!

The crease is a 9-foot (3-meter) circular area around the goal. The crease stretches from goalpost to goalpost. Beware! Offensive players cannot enter the crease. It is illegal for offensive players to be in the crease, interfering with the goalie.

Following the Rules

Men's field lacrosse is a game with many rules. It would be difficult to learn all of them, but here are some important rules to know:

- Each team must keep at least four players, including the goalie, in its defensive half of the field. There must be at least three players in the offensive half.

- Teams change sides of the field between each period, or quarter. This means that they change directions each time they change sides of the field.

- Players may run with the ball in the crosse, pass, and catch the ball. Only the goalkeeper may touch the ball with his hands when stopping a shot.

- A player may gain possession of the ball by dislodging it from an opponent's crosse with a stick check.

- If the ball or a player who has the ball goes out of bounds, the other team is awarded its possession.

- An attacking player cannot enter the crease around the goal, but he can reach in with his stick to scoop up a loose ball.

- If the goalie has the ball, he cannot be in the crease for more than five seconds.

Something Foul

When a player breaks the rules, he earns a penalty. There are two types of penalties: personal and technical fouls. When a player commits a personal foul, he is removed from the game for one to three minutes, and the other team gets the ball. The penalty for technical fouls depends on which team is in possession of the ball when the foul happens.

PERSONAL FOULS

Tripping	a player interferes with his opponent at or below the waist by using his hands, arms, feet, legs, or crosse
Unnecessary Roughness	using his stick or body, a player strikes an opponent with violent force
Illegal Crosse	a player uses a crosse that does not meet the standards
Unsportsmanlike Conduct	when a player or coach's behavior is unfavorable to the other team, including bad language or gestures, taunting, or arguing

TECHNICAL FOULS

Holding   a player interferes with the movement of his opponent or his opponent's crosse

Interference   an offensive player makes contact with a defensive player, blocking him from the person that the defensive player is defending

Offsides   a team does not have three players on its offensive side of the midfield line or at least four players on its defensive side of the midfield line

Pushing   a player shoves an opponent from behind

No Limits

Have you ever seen a football field? A football field has lines that mark the boundaries of the field. All football fields are the same size. In women's lacrosse, the field size varies, and the playing area does not have measured boundaries.

The maximum playing area is 140 yards (128 m) by 70 yards (64 m). The minimum playing area is 116 yards (106 m) by 60 yards (55 m). The goals must be placed no more than 101 yards (92 m) apart and no less than 90 yards (82 m) apart—measured from goal line to goal line. There are two goal lines, one at each end of the field. The goal lines run the width of the field and mark the end of the field.

A solid line, called the restraining line, must be marked 30 yards (27 m) from each goal line. The restraining lines divide the offensive and defensive areas of the field. Look at the diagram to learn the names and different parts of the women's lacrosse field.

12 meter fan

goal

critical scoring area

8 meter arc

goal circle

restraining line

center of field

restraining line

12 meter fan

8 meter arc

goal circle

goal

critical scoring area

It's a Girl's World

Women's lacrosse games are divided into halves. College games last for 60 minutes, with each half lasting 30 minutes. In high school, women's games last 50 minutes, with 25-minute halves. Each team is allowed one timeout per half.

Every women's lacrosse game begins with a draw at the center of the field. One player from each team raises her crosse into a horizontal position. The referee blows the whistle and places the ball between the two raised crosses. Each player raises her crosse and tries to take possession of the ball for her team. The team with the ball becomes the offense.

In women's lacrosse, each team is allowed 12 players on the field: a goalkeeper, five attackers, and six defenders. All of the players for each team work together to move the ball around the field and score goals.

Dressed to Win

Women's lacrosse is a noncontact sport. This means that players are not allowed to hit or charge their opponents with their body, making the game less dangerous than men's lacrosse. As a result, women's players do not need to wear protective pads, like men do, but women's lacrosse still requires special equipment to help them play the game.

The women's lacrosse uniform has two parts: a blouse and a skirt similar to the type female tennis players wear. These are sometimes called "skorts" because they have shorts built into them. Female players may also wear shorts in more casual games.

Players wear special shoes called cleats that give them traction while they run on the field.

Some players wear gloves to protect their hands.

Like men's lacrosse, the crosse, or stick, is made of plastic and lightweight metal. The pocket is molded and not as deep as the men's pocket. Players must carry the ball by cradling it.

The ball is made of solid rubber and must be yellow. The ball weighs about 5 ounces (140 g) and is 8 inches (20 cm) around.

All players must wear goggles to protect their eyes. This is mandatory.

Finding Your Home

Women's field lacrosse has five offensive players known as attackers. Each attacker has a different responsibility on the field and plays a different position. Here are the four types of offensive players:

First Home: The first home's job is to score goals. She plays in front of the goal and must constantly adjust her position. The first home either moves toward the goal to shoot and score or away from the goal to make room for another player on her team who has a better shot. She should have excellent stickwork.

Second Home: The second home must be able to shoot well from every angle and distance around the goal. She is an important part of moving the ball into scoring position and scoring goals. Because the second home is so important, she is often called the playmaker.

Third Home: The third home moves the ball from the defense to the attack, or offense. She must be able to feed, or pass, the ball to other players on the field. She also fills in the wing areas.

Attack Wings: Each team has two attack wings. The wings are responsible for transitioning, or moving, the ball from the defense to the attack. Each attack wing should be ready to receive the ball from the defense and run or pass the ball. Wings need to have good speed and endurance to do their job well.

Cover Your Woman

What stops a strong offense from scoring? A good defense. Women's lacrosse has six defensive positions. The defenders try to stop the attackers from scoring and gain possession of the ball for their team.

Point: The point guard is responsible for guarding, or marking, the first home. She should be able to stick check and block passes.

Coverpoint: The coverpoint is responsible for guarding the second home. She must run fast and have good footwork to play her position well.

Third Man: The third man marks the third home. She blocks passes and clears the ball.

Center: The center controls the draw. She is responsible for gaining possession of the ball for her team at each draw. She also plays both defense and attack, or offense. The center covers a large amount of the field, must be quick, and must have good endurance.

Defense Wings: Each team has two defensive wings. The defense wings guard the attack wings. They also bring the ball into the attack area.

Goalkeeper: The goalkeeper, or goalie, is responsible for protecting the goal. She stops the opposing team from scoring and helps direct the defense around the goal area. She should have courage and confidence, defending the goal well.

Do or Don't

Women's lacrosse is also a game of many rules. Here are some of the most important rules for you to know:

• Before each game begins, the referee checks every player's stick to make sure that it is legal. The most common illegal stick has a pocket that is too deep.

• If the ball enters a dangerous or unplayable area, the referee blows the whistle to stop the game. The player that has the ball or is closest to it gains its possession. When the referee blows a second whistle, play resumes.

• All players must stop all forward movement when the referee blows the whistle.

• Stick checking is not allowed when it is directed toward a player's head or face or is uncontrolled.

- Defensive players may not remain in the 8 $\frac{3}{4}$-yard (8-m) arc for more than three seconds without guarding an opposing player.

- If the ball is on the ground, a player may not cover the ball with the back of a stick's net, preventing play by another player.

- No player is allowed to touch the ball with her hands, except the goalie when she is in the goal circle.

Major and Minor

Like men's lacrosse, players earn penalties for illegal moves in women's lacrosse. The two types of penalties in women's lacrosse are called major and minor fouls. The type of foul committed by a player determines whether it is major or minor. Here are some of the most common major and minor fouls in women's lacrosse:

MAJOR FOULS

Blocking	a defender makes contact with an opponent, moving into the path of an opponent that has the ball, without allowing her a chance to move or change direction
Charging	a player charges or pushes an opponent with her hand or body
Dangerous Shot	a player makes an uncontrolled shot at the goal, goalie, or a field player
Misconduct	a player acts in a rough, dangerous, or unsportsmanlike manner, or endangers the safety of other players

MINOR FOULS

Goal Circle Fouls	when any part of an offensive or defensive player's body or crosse enters the goal circle
Empty Crosse Check	a player cannot check an opponent's crosse unless the opponent has the ball
Body Ball	when the ball hits a player's body, allowing her to gain an unfair advantage in the game

Talking the Talk

Have you ever "ripped rope" through "the pipes?" Like most sports, the game of lacrosse has many special terms. Read below to learn the the lingo of field lacrosse:

the cage: the goal

the pipes: the bars around the goal

wand: the crosse or stick

walk the dog: when a player carries the ball with one hand out in front of him or her

ripping rope: when a player scores

wormburner: a shot that rolls across the ground

give and go: a two-player offensive move

yard sale: a defensive player stick checks an offensive player that has the ball, making him or her drop the stick

the stripes: the referee

slide: a defensive player moves toward an offensive player

wheels: a player runs fast, using his or her "wheels"

ankle breaker: a very quick turn

around the world: a behind-the-back shot; the shot comes from over the shoulder of the shooting hand

black hole: a player that is a ball hog

bullet or cookie: the ball

dinger: a powerful shot that scores

egg: a soft shot

laxer: lacrosse player

The Pros

North America has two professional lacrosse organizations: the National Lacrosse League and Major League Lacrosse. The National Lacrosse League (NLL) was founded in the mid-1980s with six teams. As of 2005, 11 teams participated in the NLL. The National Lacrosse League is an indoor league and players follow the rules for indoor box lacrosse.

Major League Lacrosse (MLL) was created in 2001. The MLL is an outdoor field lacrosse league. Originally, six teams competed in the league. As of 2005, seven teams participated in the MLL.

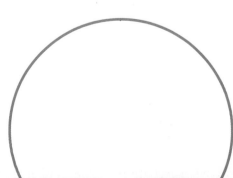

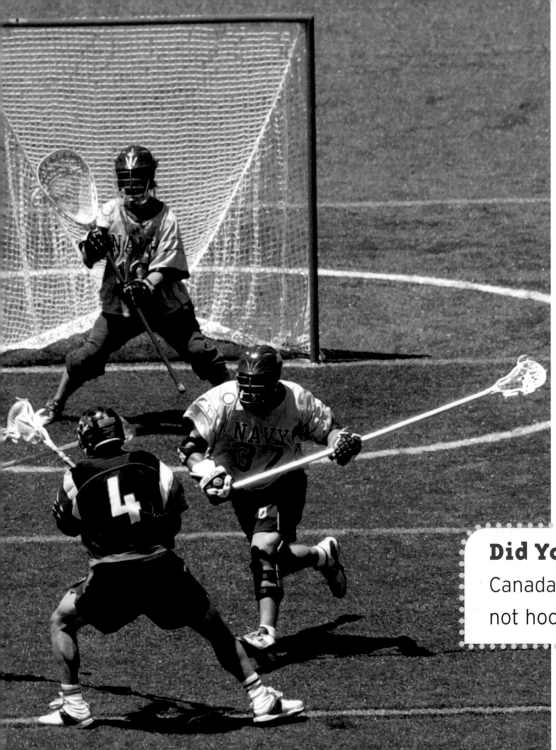

Besides the pros, North America also has many youth, high school, college, and club teams. Men's and women's field lacrosse is a popular sport that keeps expanding every year. Club teams allow players that are not in high school, college, or the pros to continue playing lacrosse. Each region of the United States has several club teams.

Did You Know?

Canada's national sport is lacrosse, not hockey.

Spanning the Globe

The International Lacrosse Federation (ILF) and the International Federation of Women's Lacrosse Association (IFWLA) are the international governing bodies of men's and women's lacrosse.

The ILF was founded in 1974. It has a mission to promote and develop the game of lacrosse all over the world. Today, members from 20 nations participate in men's lacrosse games sponsored by the ILF.

The IFWLA was formed in 1972 to further develop the game of women's lacrosse across the globe. Australia, England, Scotland, Wales, and the United States were the original members of the IFWLA. As of 2005, 10 member nations participated in IFWLA competitions.

Future Lacrosse Stars

Youth lacrosse is one of the most rapid growing sports. In the United States, 67 percent of all lacrosse players participate in youth lacrosse!

Playing to Win

The World Cup

International competition has been a tradition in men's lacrosse since 1860. In 1974, the ILF started the Men's World Lacrosse Championship, which is now held every four years. The IFWLA held the first Women's World Lacrosse Championship in 1982. The championship competitions are each known as the World Cup. Each country that plays in the World Cup has a national team that represents its nation.

The NCAA Championships

Every year, college teams participate in the National Collegiate Athletic Association (NCAA) Men's and Women's Lacrosse Championships. The NCAA Championships are becoming popular in the United States. In the last 10 years, the number of fans that attend the outdoor lacrosse championships has nearly tripled. Recently the men's outdoor championship game had a crowd of nearly 38,000 people. That crowd set a record for the largest to ever attend an NCAA outdoor championship game!

What Happened When?

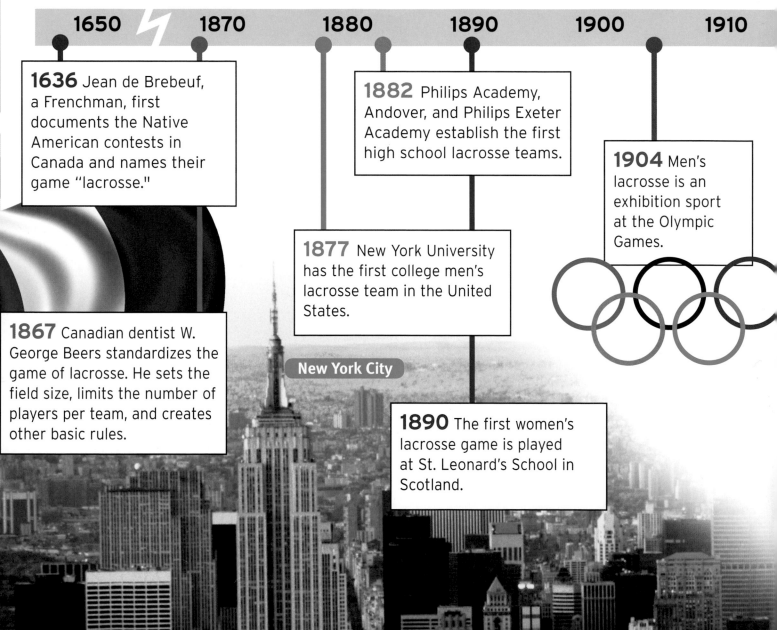

1650   **1870**   **1880**   **1890**   **1900**   **1910**

1636 Jean de Brebeuf, a Frenchman, first documents the Native American contests in Canada and names their game "lacrosse."

1882 Philips Academy, Andover, and Philips Exeter Academy establish the first high school lacrosse teams.

1904 Men's lacrosse is an exhibition sport at the Olympic Games.

1877 New York University has the first college men's lacrosse team in the United States.

1867 Canadian dentist W. George Beers standardizes the game of lacrosse. He sets the field size, limits the number of players per team, and creates other basic rules.

New York City

1890 The first women's lacrosse game is played at St. Leonard's School in Scotland.

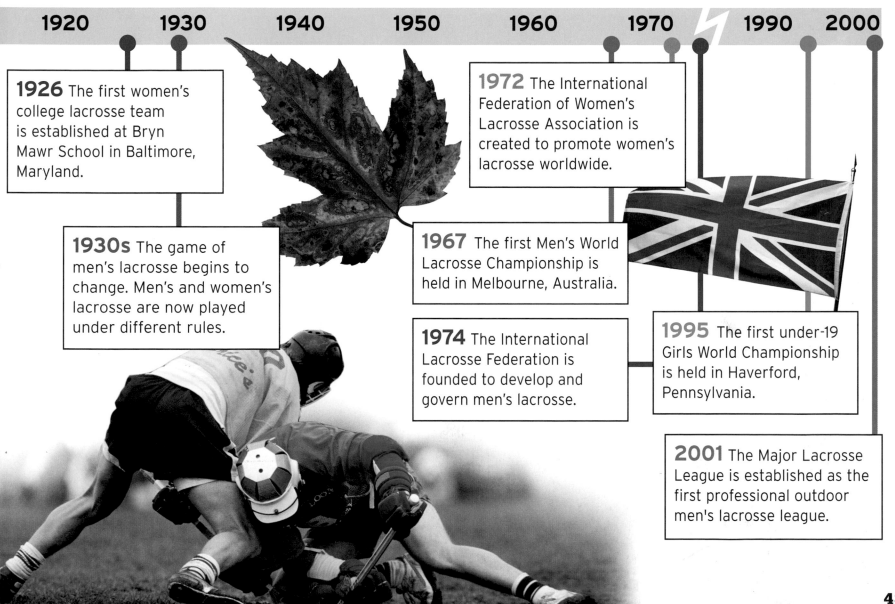

1920   1930   1940   1950   1960   1970   1990   2000

1926 The first women's college lacrosse team is established at Bryn Mawr School in Baltimore, Maryland.

1930s The game of men's lacrosse begins to change. Men's and women's lacrosse are now played under different rules.

1972 The International Federation of Women's Lacrosse Association is created to promote women's lacrosse worldwide.

1967 The first Men's World Lacrosse Championship is held in Melbourne, Australia.

1974 The International Lacrosse Federation is founded to develop and govern men's lacrosse.

1995 The first under-19 Girls World Championship is held in Haverford, Pennsylvania.

2001 The Major Lacrosse League is established as the first professional outdoor men's lacrosse league.

Fun Lacrosse Facts

Native Americans call lacrosse "The Creator's Game."

What does cooking have to do with lacrosse? A player that is not a good cradler and just runs down the field is called a frying pan. This is his or her nickname because he or she carries the stick like a "frying pan."

Players that devote all of their time and life to playing lacrosse are known as "laxheads."

"Popcorn" is a shot put directly into the goalie's stick.

Lacrosse is one of the fastest growing sports in the United States. Youth membership (15 and under) has doubled since 1999 to more than 60,000 participants.

A "submarine" is an underhand shot.

More than 15,000 high school women play lacrosse every year.

45

Lacrosse Words to Know

artificial turf: a material that looks like grass; also known as carpet

boundary: the limit of the field

crease: the circular area around the goal

defense: when the team tries to stop the offense from scoring

goal: a point scored; also the netted area into which the ball must land to score a goal

goalkeeper: the player who guards the net and keeps the ball from entering the goal; also known as the goalie

offense: when the team has the ball and tries to score goals

noncontact: players are not allowed to hit or charge their opponents

penalty: a punishment for breaking the rules

pocket: the mesh in the head of the stick that catches, holds, and directs the ball when passing or shooting

referee: the official who calls the penalties and handles the face-offs and draws on the field

stick check: a defensive move that hits the ball carrier's stick to try to dislodge the ball

stickwork: the way a player moves or handles his crosse, or stick

timeout: when a team stops play during the game, usually for a short period

Metric Conversion
1 yard = .9144 meters

GLOSSARY

Other Words to Know

coordination: ability to move your body and muscles easily

dislodge: to force out of a place or thing

endanger: to put another person at risk of harm or injury

horizontal: parallel to the ground

interfere: to get in the way of an opponent

protective: something that keeps you more safe so you do not get hurt

strategy: a plan or method to do something

vary: different from one another

Where To Learn More

AT THE LIBRARY

Crossingham, John, and Katherine Kantor. *Lacrosse in Action*. New York: Crabtree Publishing Company, 2002.

McCoy, Lisa, and Susan Saliba. *Lacrosse*. Broomall, Pa.: Mason Crest Publishers, 2003.

ON THE ROAD

The Lacrosse Museum & National Hall of Fame
113 W. University Parkway
Baltimore, MD 21210
410/235-6882

ON THE WEB

For more information on LACROSSE, use FactHound to track down Web sites related to this book.

1. Go to www.facthound.com
2. Type in this book ID: 0756516854
3. Click on the *Fetch It* button.

Your trusty FactHound will fetch the best Web sites for you!

INDEX

ABOUT THE AUTHOR

Sandra Will graduated magna cum laude from Barnard College, Columbia University, with a degree in English Literature. Sandra's passion for sports stems from her childhood. When she is not watching a game, she enjoys reading books, visiting museums, and playing with her dog, Maggie. Originally from Chehalis, Washington, Sandra lives in New York City.